# The Graphic Art of Winslow Homer

Organized by

THE MUSEUM OF GRAPHIC ART

New York

*Participating Museums*

Achenbach Foundation for Graphic Arts

The Akron Art Institute

Bowdoin College Museum of Art

Cincinnati Art Museum

The Detroit Institute of Arts

Everson Museum of Art

The Fine Arts Gallery of San Diego

The Minneapolis Institute of Arts

The Museum of Fine Arts, Houston

National Collection of Fine Arts,

Smithsonian Institution

Oklahoma Art Center

The Parrish Art Museum

Santa Barbara Museum of Art

University of Kansas Museum of Art

Whitney Museum of American Art

1968—1970

# The Graphic Art of Winslow Homer

by Lloyd Goodrich

Foreword by
Donald H. Karshan

Published for
The Museum of Graphic Art
by the
Smithsonian Institution Press

*First printing 1968*

*Designed and produced by Chanticleer Press, Inc.*
*Printed by Amilcare Pizzi, S. p. A., Milano, Italy.*

# Contents

# Foreword

The prints of Winslow Homer, America's most celebrated artist, have periodically been exhibited but an extensive retrospective of his graphics, seen in the context of his overall artistic development, has never before been undertaken. Nor, for that matter, has a publication been devoted solely to the analysis of the full range of his graphic *oeuvre*. The Museum of Graphic Art, in the present exhibition and monograph, addresses itself to that task. The retrospective, by far the most ambitious presentation of Homer's graphic art, comprises all of his etchings, his most important lithographs, many of his most striking wood engravings, and related paintings and drawings.

The entire scope of the exhibition is preserved in this publication. Nearly all of the works in the retrospective are reproduced, using the monogravure process in order to approximate the originals as closely as possible. Paintings, watercolors and drawings that are related to certain prints are juxtaposed to those prints for comparative study. It is hoped that the exhibition and this publication will establish Homer, long admired for his paintings, as a major figure in the history of American printmaking.

Lloyd Goodrich, Advisory Director of the Whitney Museum of American Art and the foremost authority on Homer, served as consultant to The Museum of Graphic Art in the formulation of the exhibition, and wrote the text for this publication. Mr. Goodrich's devotion to Homer over several decades and his unceasing investigation into the artist's life and work serve as a model for art historians and students of American art.

In the absence of a comprehensive exhibition and publication, two principal misunderstandings regarding Homer's graphic art have flourished. One is that Homer's etchings are simply black and white reproductions of his paintings and the other is that his wood engravings are pedestrian interpretations made by professional cutters and far removed from Homer's original designs. These conclusions tend to diminish our appreciation and understanding of this artist's graphic work. One of the principal objectives of The Museum of Graphic Art, therefore, is to clarify these points with this exhibition and the helpful explanations of Mr. Goodrich.

As part of a series designed to cover major printmakers, "The Graphic Art of Winslow Homer" is the second comprehensive exhibition and publication by The Museum of Graphic Art. The first dealt with the graphic art of Mary Cassatt. Both exhibitions were planned for national tours; the publications based on them should carry the works to an even wider audience.

The Board of Directors of The Museum of Graphic Art acknowledges the extensive assistance given by the many museums and private collectors by their generous, long-term loans. Grateful acknowledgement is also made to Mr. Lloyd Goodrich for his invaluable contributions, to Mrs. Goodrich and Miss Linda Harsh for their patient and thoughtful assistance, and to the directors, curators and staffs of the fifteen participating museums.

DONALD H. KARSHAN
President, The Museum of Graphic Art

# The Graphic Art of Winslow Homer

Winslow Homer began his career as a graphic artist, and essentially he remained one all his life. Until he was over twenty-six his work was almost entirely in black and white—lithography, illustration and drawing. Only when he was approaching twenty-seven did he begin to paint regularly, and until he was nearly forty he carried on a double career of painting and illustration. And throughout his life his style retained a basic graphic character; even his latest oils and watercolors were built on a foundation of draftsmanship.

Homer was essentially self-taught. His training was in the actual practice of his profession. At about nineteen he was apprenticed to the Boston lithographic firm of John H. Bufford. His first job was designing illustrated covers for popular songs, some of them copied from photographs, or from earlier designs such as "The Ratcatcher's Daughter" (pl. 1), adapted from a music sheet published in London. Bufford soon discovered that he had an apprentice of unusual skill, and turned over to him the more demanding pictorial designs. One of the most ambitious was a large lithograph of the entire Massachusetts Senate, forty-two individual portraits, probably from photographs—a remarkably able work for a youth of twenty (pl. 3). But Homer was already exceptionally independent and strong-willed; and even though he smuggled his initials on to as many stones as he could, the hackwork at Bufford's was slavery to him. As his first biographer, George W. Sheldon, wrote later: "His sojourn there was a treadmill existence. Two years at that grindstone unfitted him for further bondage." When his apprenticeship was up, on his twenty-first birthday, in February 1857, he left Bufford's and began his career of illustrator.

In those days before photo-mechanical processes, the usual method of reproducing illustrations in magazines and books was wood-engraving. The wood block (boxwood because of its fine grain) was polished and coated with white, making a surface almost as smooth as paper. On this the artist drew his picture, in reverse. The block was then turned over to an engraver, who cut away the bare white parts of the surface, leaving the drawn lines in relief, to be printed like type. The drawing itself had been destroyed piecemeal in the process. The functions of artist and engraver were completely separate; as far as we know, Homer never cut his own blocks. Sometimes reportorial magazine artists sent in only sketches, to be redrawn by staff artists. Judging by the style of Homer's illustrations, he almost invariably drew them on the block himself.

Homer's first magazine illustrations appeared in June 1857 in the staid Boston periodical *Ballou's Pictorial Drawing-Room Companion,* and two months later in the prestigious new magazine *Harper's Weekly* of New York. Soon he was an active contributor to both. In the fall of 1859, when *Ballou's* was about to give up illustrations, he moved to New York. *Harper's* made him a tempting offer to become a staff artist. "I declined it," Homer later told Sheldon, "because I had had a taste of freedom. The slavery at Bufford's was too fresh in my recollection to let me care to bind myself again. From the time that I took my nose off that lithographic stone, I have had no master; and never shall have any." But he continued to work for the magazine as a free lance.

When the Civil War broke out, *Harper's* sent him to the Virginia front several times as "our special artist." But he was not permanently assigned to the seat of war, and most of his war illustrations were done back in New York from drawings made in Virginia. Actual fighting was seldom shown; mostly he pictured everyday camp life, seen with a fresh eye, utter truthfulness, keen characterization, and a sense of humor. No other magazine artist drew such candid portraits of how the Yankees actually looked and behaved. On the other hand, his few battle scenes captured the violence of combat with unidealized realism and immediacy (pl. 7, 8).

The war furnished material for a brief return to lithography in a series of "Campaign Sketches" drawn on stone by Homer in 1863 for the Boston publisher Louis Prang (pl. 13–20). Here again were the daily incidents and humors of army life. In their first-hand observation and graphic skill they were close to his drawings made at the front, of which a large collection is now in the Cooper Union Museum, New York. One of the virtues of the lithographs is that they present Homer's graphic quality directly, without the sometimes deadening interposition of the wood-engraver. In December 1863 we find Homer writing to Prang: "I have seen a copy of 'Campaign Sketches.' The cover is very neat and the pictures look better than they would in color, but why did you not get a copyright?" Next year Homer and Prang followed up with a series of small souvenir cards such as were popular in those days: "Life in Camp," twenty-four in all, more burlesque in humor and cruder in handling (pl. 21–24). "Our Special" is a caricature bearing little resemblance to Homer, but the soldier in "Good Bye" is himself.

That his lithographic crayon was not entirely idle in peacetime subjects is revealed by the delightful large print of "Union Pond, Williamsburgh, Long Island" (pl. 4). Though his name does not appear on it (a frequent practice of the time) the figures are unquestionably by him, not only because of their graphic style but their parallels with figures in other works. (The buildings are probably by another hand.) He was also responsible for another large lithograph, "Skating on Central Park, New York," published by Bufford in 1861, which reproduces Homer's watercolor now in the City Art Museum of St. Louis; but the drawing on the stone is not characteristic of him.

After the war Homer in both paintings and illustrations devoted himself to the subject matter that meant most to him—country life. From boyhood he had loved the outdoor world, and this love was to continue and grow throughout his life, and to play a dominating part in his work. Although he lived in New York over twenty years, he never painted it, and seldom even illustrated city scenes except at the beginning of his career.

One half of Homer's rural world was that of the summer resort, with women playing the leading roles. Although he was to remain a bachelor all his life, his youthful work reveals a devotion to female comeliness and a keen eye for fashion. His women are always young and goodlooking, engaged in the few outdoor activities allowed to the sex in those tight-corseted days. He delighted in their hoopskirts, puffed sleeves, flying ribbons, fringed parasols, and all the other feminine extravagances of that rococo period, and few artists made more out of them pictorially. He can almost be said to have invented the American Girl, and the illustrations and paintings in which she figured were the most engaging visual records of fashionable American country life in the 1860's and 1870's.

The other half of his rural world was that of the deep country and the old-fashioned Yankee farm. In a day when most American artists depicted farm life with nostalgic idealization, Homer's uncouth figures and homely settings carried the conviction of utter authenticity. Yet underlying his honest naturalism was a strain of pastoral poetry, a love of country life at its simplest and most primitive—life spent close to nature, ruled by the cycle of the seasons. This combination of reserved poetry and unsweetened realism gave Homer's country pictures a flavor unique in the art of the time.

Children played a central part in these rustic scenes, pictured with complete sympathy but no trace of the mawkish sentimentality of the period. Homer had retained a boy's sense of delight in the freedom of outdoor life, and his pictures of children exploring the pleasures of farm and seashore and mountains combine matter-of-fact realism with a lyrical sense of the early-morning freshness of childhood in the country.

Until he was close to forty Homer continued to support himself largely by illustrating, mostly for *Harper's Weekly* but also for a number of other magazines, and for book publishers. As time passed, his contributions ceased to be illustrations in the usual sense. They were no longer reportorial or humorous, or necessarily related to a text. They were independent pictures, as purely works of art as his paintings. Indeed they were sometimes actually reproductions of his paintings (pl. 10, 66 and 68, and 76).

In the 1870's photography was beginning to be used in wood-engraving; the artist's drawing could be transferred photographically on to the wood block, and the engraver could keep the original in sight while he worked. But in Homer's case the absence of any originals identical with the illustrations seems to indicate that he did not use this method. Even in the illustrations reproducing his paintings, the changes show that he himself must have redrawn them on the block. This appears to be true of even such an exact reproduction as "Snap-the-whip" (pl. 68), judging by the drawing (pl. 67), which corresponds in size with the wood-engraving, and was probably used in tracing the picture on the block.

Although none of Homer's wood blocks have been found (they were probably planed down for re-use, just as lithographic stones are ground down), the visual character of his illustrations, and the technique of his few preliminary studies for them, indicate that his drawings on the block were probably in pencil or crayon, with some ink wash—somewhere between line drawing and black and white watercolor.

In wood-engraving, which is essentially the same graphic medium as type, the impression of all the inked areas is in flat black; and this very flatness offers definite decorative possibilities. While basically a line medium, wood-engraving can reproduce tones by minute parallel lines; and the engravers of Homer's day performed technical miracles in translating tones into the lines of the block. But to retain its artistic integrity, wood-engraving must retain the integrity of its flat and linear nature. Practised by artists who understood this, it could be a beautiful medium. Homer was definitely one of these. His early illustrations were largely in line, with some subsidiary tone. As he developed he used tone more and more. But he seldom lost sight of the basic physical character of the medium. The picture was built on a strong linear foundation, with tone used as an enrichment but remaining subordinate. Outlines were strong, the forms were simplified into broad masses, and the areas of light and shadow were sharply defined.

Homer's early style, in his paintings and drawings as well as his illustrations, was that of a direct observer of nature, relying on his own eyes rather than on what he had learned from other art. He saw the motif in big patterns of lights and darks, and he recorded it that way, directly and boldly. This primal freshness of vision had marked his style from the first. But it was combined with an innate sense of decorative values. For him line and tone were not only means of representing what he saw; they had their own sensuous quality. He had an instinctive feeling for pattern, for rhythmic line, for the balance of darks and lights and middle tones.

This decorative quality has interesting parallels with Japanese art—an influence that probably first reached him through his close friend John La Farge, who was collecting Japanese prints early in the 1860's. There are also parallels with the current work of the young French impressionists. There is a theory that the Japanese and impressionist influences came to Homer in the ten months he spent in France in 1866–67. But these parallels had already appeared in paintings and illustrations done before his French visit: for example, the beautifully designed "Our National Winter Exercise—Skating," in January 1866 (pl. 25). Homer's Orientalism was never an articulate aesthetic, as with Whistler; it was a basic affinity in visual response to nature. Like the Japanese printmakers, he saw nature in patterns of masses and lines, lights and darks. To him there was no conflict between naturalism and decorative values.

Homer's best illustrations were products of conscious, thoughtful design. Frequently they were made up of elements from two or more pictures already executed in other mediums. Several examples of this are given in the plate section of the present publication. "Shipbuilding, Gloucester Harbor," for example, made use of two oils and a watercolor to create a composition more complex than any of them (pl. 72–75). "The Summit of Mount Washington" combined two oils of different years and sizes (pl. 39–41). The four examples of this procedure given in our plates (pl. 39–41, 63–65, 69–71, 72–75) could be multiplied many times. Homer was a prolific artist, but he was also an economical one; and usable concepts were not wasted by him. His culminating achievements were the illustrations in *Harper's Weekly* in 1873 and 1874, many of them making use of his watercolors of these years. They were among the most consciously and finely designed of all his works, comparable to the best of his mature paintings and etchings.

At the height of his powers as an illustrator, Homer stopped. After 1874 there was only one illustration in *Harper's* and only a few elsewhere. His reasons, like much in his personal life, are not known. The most probable is that in the summer of 1873 he had taken up a new medium, watercolor, was painting many watercolors every summer, and last but not least, was finding a ready sale for them. In any case, watercolor, also a graphic medium in the broadest sense, took the place of illustration from then on.

In his middle forties Homer's life and art took a new direction. In 1881 and 1882 he spent almost two years in England, near Tynemouth, a fishing port on the North Sea. Working mostly in watercolor, he concentrated on the subjects that were to dominate his work thenceforth—the sea, and those who make their living on it. The grim North Sea with its constant storms and shipwrecks, and the hardihood of the Tynemouth fishermen and fish-wives, brought a new seriousness to his art. His fashionable young ladies were replaced by robust fishergirls, doing men's work; and in his pictures they were given an heroic strength and dignity. These English watercolors when exhibited after his return brought him increasing recognition.

The year after his return, in 1883, Homer left New York for good and settled on a lonely point of land on the Maine coast, Prout's Neck. Here he was to live the rest of his life, and here his art came to full maturity. His themes now were the sea, the forest and the mountains, and the lives of outdoor men—sailors, fishermen and hunters. With each year his work gained in strength, substance and skill.

The first products of this growth, from 1884 to 1886, were a series of sea paintings featuring man's battle against the force and danger of the sea. They were definitely story-telling pictures, but unlike the sentimental anecdotes prevalent at the time, they possessed elemental human meaning. Serious, often tragic, they had an almost Biblical earnestness and simplicity. Their dramatic quality and realistic power soon won them a permanent place among pictorial epics of the sea.

These sea paintings were highly popular with the public and with critics and collectors. When the first of them, "The Life Line" (pl. 89), was exhibited at the National Academy in February 1884, it was bought on the opening day for $2,500 by the prominent collector Catharine Lorillard Wolfe—her first American acquisition. Two months later *The New York News* reported: "Winslow Homer is making a large etching of his picture 'The Life Line.'" This was the first of a series of etchings based on his sea paintings and his English watercolors, doubtless motivated by their popularity and by his desire to reach a wide audience. The medium was not entirely new to him, as shown by his charming little print,

"Girl Posing in a Chair" (pl. 87), which can be dated about 1876 from similarities to certain watercolors and drawings (the same girl and the same chair). But now he was undertaking etching as a major medium. The eight finished plates he etched between 1884 and 1889 form a unique phase in his lifework.

Homer later told his friend John W. Beatty that he had never taken lessons in etching, but had read books and talked to friends who made prints, and worked things out for himself. The man from whom he learned most was his printer George W. H. Ritchie, himself an etcher, who had a shop in New York which Homer frequented when he was in town. Ritchie's assistant and successor Charles S. White, who printed many of Homer's plates, and with whom I talked in 1941, told me that in the shop Homer met fellow etchers, including J. Alden Weir and Carleton Wiggins, who gave him advice. White said that when Homer was in Maine, Ritchie would prepare his plates and send them to him; that Homer would bite them himself, but having no press, would send them to Ritchie for professional proofing, and when finished for lettering and printing. In a letter from Prout's Neck to Ritchie in October 1888 Homer wrote of a plate he was working on: "It promises to be worthy of your pupil, which is more than I can say of some of my recent work. There has been altogether too much bragging for the small amount of creditable work." A few days later he reported: "I have bitten my plate today. It took six hours with 20 minutes for the first line to go by. I think it is very fine. . . . If this turns out as good as I think, it is a mere echo of what I have seen you do, and I wish to assure you that I am most grateful to you."

"The Life Line" is a fairly close reproduction of the painting; the central figures of the unconscious woman and the sailor who is rescuing her in a breeches buoy are almost identical (pl. 89, 90). But there are changes. The composition has been cut down at the top and sides, eliminating the ship's sail and much of the sea and cliff, so that the figures are larger in proportion to the whole. Otherwise the main features are very close. This raises the question of how Homer reproduced his original paintings and watercolors so exactly (though with changes, as we shall see). In all but two cases ("The Life Line" and "A Voice from the Cliffs") the known history of the pictures makes it probable that they were still in his possession. In the case of "The Life Line" he may have started the etching before the painting left him, or he may have copied it in the Academy show, or he may have had a photograph of it, by himself or someone else. Recent research by Philip C. Beam, published in his *Winslow Homer at Prout's Neck*, indicates that at least later Homer used a camera.

He evidently worked long over this first larger plate; successive proofs show more and more lines added, especially in the woman's figure. As a result the final state, compared to his later etchings, is labored, stiff and dark. Most of the prints were in dark green ink, perhaps to suggest the color of stormy water—not an altogether happy idea.

When painting "The Life Line" Homer had conceived a similar picture of rescue from the sea, "Undertow" (pl. 91). Begun in 1883, it was not finished until 1886, and first exhibited in early 1887. Probably some time during these years he etched a small plate (pl. 92), evidently first making an experimental plate of studies of heads (pl. 88). The final version of "Undertow," of which only two prints are known, shows only the two women, not the men rescuing them. Much of the sky and water are omitted, so that the print gives a much larger role to the figures, even more than in "The Life Line."

In 1887 Homer etched his largest plate so far, based on his oil, "Eight Bells," the smallest and least dramatic of his deep-sea paintings but in some ways the finest (pl. 93). These two bearded sailors, going about their immemorial duties amid the tumbled waste of waters, have an heroic simplicity and strength—figures symbolic of man's courage and skill matched against the power of the ocean. This sense of the universal and the timeless makes "Eight Bells" one of the enduring classics of the sea.

The etching (pl. 94) is almost as large. Again he has increased the scale of the figures, making them more dominant, and creating a stronger black and white pattern—a device he used in all his etchings based on paintings. In "Eight Bells" he also cut off much of the right side, so that the two figures are not centered, resulting in an asymmetrical composition that gives more space to the waves and an increased sense of the vast expanse of the ocean. There are other slight changes, such as the center figure leaning more to the right, that are almost imperceptible but improve the relations of part to part. Here, as in all his etchings, the print is not merely a copy of the painting; it is a re-creating of the subject in another medium. The drawing throughout is not that of a copyist but of a graphic artist building his forms anew, and in some ways more surely. When one examines details like the waves and clouds, one sees that Homer has shaped them more decisively and vigorously in the etching. This is a basic difference between his prints and the relatively dry, mechanical reproductions of his paintings by other etchers of the time.

With each succeeding plate Homer's technical skill was increasing; by the time he did "Eight Bells" he was handling the complications of biting and stopping out as though he had been doing them all his life. It is true that he did not attempt the nuances of the medium as Whistler and his followers were doing: refinements of values, skillful printing methods, wiping the plate or leaving areas fully inked so as to achieve subtle variations of tone. Homer's etchings were constructed primarily in pure line, the forms being built by linear modelling, the darks secured by linework rather than by tonal printing. The devices of printing that the new school of etchers was exploiting had little place in his work, which belonged to an older tradition, akin to engraving. Compared to the subtleties and refinements of the new men, his style was severe and hard. But no other American etcher of the period displayed his structural strength, his mastery of the human figure, and his completeness of design.

By 1888 Homer was fully engrossed in etching; to this year belong three plates: "Perils of the Sea," "Mending the Tears" and "A Voice from the Cliffs." In them he went back from his recent oils to his Tynemouth watercolors. It is interesting to note that all three were reversed in relation to the originals, which had not been true of "The Life Line" and "Eight Bells." His reasons for this are not known, but since an etching plate prints in reverse, it was of course more practical in working from an original to make the plate read the same way. The oil versions of "The Life Line" and "Eight Bells" were current or recent works, well-known and publicly exhibited or about to be, so that it would not have been advisable to reverse them, whereas the three watercolors were seven to five years old. (The reversed etching of "Undertow" was so different from the painting that he could have felt no need to make the figures agree.) Similarly, his earlier wood-engraved reproductions of oils (pl. 10, 68) had also read the same way as the originals; but "Gathering Berries" had been reversed from the watercolor (pl. 82, 83).

In "Perils of the Sea" (pl. 98) the composition though reversed is substantially the same as in the watercolor (pl. 97), but he has eliminated the railing and the outflung arm of the fisherman, thus giving the tragic figures of the two waiting women greater prominence and poignancy. (His first proof is inscribed in his hand: "O hear us when we cry to thee / For those in peril on the sea. / 267. Hymnal.") The etching is more tonal than most of his, but the tones are created by fine intricate lines, as in the ominous clouds and the seething turmoil of breaking waves.

"Mending the Tears" (pl. 96) is based on the large watercolor "Mending Nets: or, Far from Billingsgate" (pl. 95). (The new title was a sly bit of humor, since one girl is mending a torn net, the other a torn sock.) This time Homer altered the design more radically than in prints of preceding years, changing the shape from vertical to horizontal, eliminating the empty upper sky, the wall and the hanging basket, and transforming the almost blank background into space filled with tangible features—rocks, beach, boats, sea, a cloudy sky. All these changes are to the good: the forms fit more satisfyingly into the horizontal composition, and the omissions simplify the design and give greater importance to the two statuesque figures. Here as in all his etchings he has concentrated on the central elements and disposed of competing or non-essential elements. The background is no longer blank; its forms and movements are integrated with the figures. Especially noticeable is the modelling of the bodies, in fine lines going around the forms, building them solidly, and creating monumental substance and weight. Though drawn entirely in line, the forms have the roundness of sculptural relief. The suppression of local tones in clothes, flesh and hair enhances this sense. In his etchings Homer was achieving a sculptural quality that was not always present in his oils and watercolors. The head of the near girl is one of the richest, most delicate pieces of modelling in all his work.

"A Voice from the Cliffs" (pl. 100) was based on a large watercolor of 1883 (pl. 99) which in turn was a replica of his English oil of 1882, "Hark! the Lark." In etching the plate Homer probably did not have access to the watercolor, which had been sold, but he may have had the oil, and perhaps an etching of the watercolor made by James D. Smillie in 1886. Aside from the reversing of the composition, the chief changes are again in the background: he has cut off part of the top, has given the cliffs more definite and interesting shapes and instead of distant beach and water has placed the girls against a sloping rock, thereby creating a closer relation between them and their setting, and altogether a more unified design.

In 1889 Homer etched a second version of "The Life Line," titled "Saved" (pl. 103), his largest print and in many ways his finest. Here the transformation from the oil and the earlier etching is more fundamental than in any other print. Aside from reversing the figures, he has changed the entire setting from a wide view of rolling waves and distant cliff to a close-up of surf raging on nearby rocks, an image much more immediate and forceful. Instead of the roller-coaster waves of the earlier print, the breakers now create an intricate pattern, alive with movement, and in their fine design suggestive of Japanese art. They form a ground completely integrated with the figures, part of the whole picture plane. In a plastic sense this is the most unified and fully realized of all his etchings.

There are also significant changes in the figures. In the painting and the previous print the man's legs with their heavy boots were obtrusively prominent, but in "Saved" there is only a glimpse of one leg, and the man's head is covered by the flying scarf, so that he becomes a strange shrouded form, out of which two strong arms emerge, clasping the woman's body. The woman's figure is now dominant, the man's subordinate. Her body, fully revealed instead of partly shadowed as in previous versions, is one of the most completely realized forms in all his work, sculptural in its long rhythmic lines. The windblown drapery clinging to her legs takes flowing shapes that complete the whole movement of the interlocked figures. The modelling of her figure shows a linear variety and skill greater than in any of his prints. The whole picture is alive with energy and motion; few of his works are so plastic, so purely composed of form and movement. "Saved" is no mere repetition of an early picture; it is a new creation—one of his most complete works in any medium, prophetic of the finest of his mature paintings.

Homer spent the summer and early fall of 1889 in the Adirondacks, fishing, hunting, and painting many watercolors. This visit resulted in what was probably his last etching, "Fly Fishing, Saranac Lake" (pl. 102). This time he appears to have abandoned his custom of making prints out of existing pictures, and to have painted a preliminary study especially for the etching. The watercolor "Netting the Fish" (pl. 101) is in black and white, unlike any other known work of the time, and this and its closeness to the etching indicate that it was a trial run for the print. In the etching another innovation was the extensive use, in the background, of aquatint and of burnishing the plate, to create the effect of foliage, water and fallen trees, seen in a hazy, ghostlike atmosphere. This was the first time he had departed from pure linear etching to work in tone, and it reveals him experimenting with new technical methods, and exploring the fuller resources of the etching medium.

For two years printmaking had occupied most of Homer's time. No oils dated 1887 to 1889 are recorded; he painted watercolors in the first and last years, but in 1888 the only known works are etchings and a few illustrations. The sale of the prints, handled at first by Ritchie without much success, was taken over about 1887 by the print distributor C. Klackner of New York, and on August 1, 1888, Homer signed an agreement by which Klackner had exclusive publishing rights to such plates as the artist wished to turn over to him, each party to pay half the cost of paper and printing, and Homer to get half the net receipts. The larger plates were priced at $20, with prints on parchment at $30; the smaller ones at $15. Two and three years later Klackner added large photogravures of "A Voice from the Cliffs" and of a later painting, "The Signal of Distress," with a "limited edition of artist's proofs" signed by Homer, at $18. It is amusing that Klackner's circular on "Original Etchings by Winslow Homer" made no distinction between the etchings and the photogravures. (Homer himself also co-signed etchings made by other artists of his paintings, such as Hamilton Hamilton's reproduction of "The Fog Warning" in 1887.) Indeed, nothing about Homer's etchings had the preciousness usually associated with the medium. For the publisher, they were simply reproductions of popular pictures, aimed at the general public rather than the small circle of print collectors. Doubtless most of them, in golden oak frames, found their way into seaside boarding houses and doctors' offices and similar non-artistic homes. Only some years after Homer's death did they begin to be ranked as works of art. In a recent survey by the writer, of Homer etchings in museums, I found only a few that had been acquired before the 1920's.

In the beginning Homer had high hopes of financial success with his prints. In May 1888 he wrote the Boston gallery owner J. Eastman Chase: "I have an idea for next winter, if what I am now engaged on is a success, and Mr. K. is agreeable. That is to exhibit an oil-painting in a robbery-box [Homer's name for a shadow-box] with an etching from it at the end of your gallery, with a pretty girl at the desk to sell." But his hopes were not realized. In his recent book on Homer, Philip C. Beam mentions a memorandum of 1892 on the sale of twenty-one prints, which netted the artist $114.67, less than $5.50 each. Although only about a hundred of each of the five etchings handled by Klackner were printed, with a few more for the best-sellers, the editions were not sold out even by the end of the artist's life. Of "A Voice from the Cliffs," one of his largest and most ambitious etchings, he made only six prints; and two years later Klackner substituted a photogravure of the original oil. As late as the 1900's, when Homer was generally considered one of America's leading artists, and collectors were competing for his paintings, we find him writing his dealer M. Knoedler & Company: "Mr. C. Klackner has for sale *four etchings* etched by myself, at the expense of *two years time & hard work*—'The Life Line,' 'Peril on the Sea,' 'Eight Bells,' 'Mending Tears'—*all of which are very good*, and should have been put forward long ago, but C. Klackner is waiting for me to die, is my idea of the matter."

This lack of success is puzzling. It is easy to see why Homer's etchings did not appeal to print collectors and museums, who were buying Whistler and the French etchers, and would consider his style deplorably unaesthetic. But why the general public for whom they were intended did not buy more of them is harder to understand. Perhaps, as Homer said, the failure was one of marketing. And a generation used to the sweetly sentimental may have found them grim.

Probably because of this lack of response, Homer did no more etchings after 1889. This was a distinct loss to American printmaking. He had been growing steadily, using etching more and more as a creative medium. Nevertheless, this group of his etchings can be numbered among his capital works in any medium. Homer himself thought so, for in a letter of 1902 he spoke of his recent watercolors as being "as good work, with the exception of one or two etchings, as I ever did."

About 1900 the five plates in Ritchie's possession ("The Life Line," "Eight Bells," "Mending the Tears," "Perils of the Sea" and "Fly Fishing") were put in storage, and no more prints were made from them until about 1940, when the printer Charles S. White, who had bought the business from Ritchie, began to make posthumous prints. (White considered them better than those made in the Ritchie shop.) In 1941, when I met him, he still had a number of the lifetime prints, some signed by Homer. He showed me the plates, which were steel-faced, and said that they had been steel-faced when first made.

In 1941 William M. Ivins, Curator of Prints in the Metropolitan Museum of Art, bought the five plates from White; they are still owned by the Museum. Ivins had White make new prints under his direction. The lifetime prints from the Ritchie shop had been in the somewhat romantic printing style of the period, with a good deal of ink left in the darks, so that the effect was tonal as well as linear. Ivins told me that he asked White to wipe the plates clean to secure a dryer, more linear and more structural quality. Of "Eight Bells," for example, the Metropolitan has four prints: one lifetime print, with a good deal of ink in the figures, making them stand out dark and strongly contrasted against the sea and sky; and three prints made by White in 1941: one in the same style, and two under Ivins' direction, with the plate relatively clean, no extra tone in the figures, the lines clear and sharp. The result is a little dry, but stronger and more solid; the figures, which formerly were dark silhouetted shapes, holes in the picture plane, now stand out in relief. (Our reproductions, incidentally, are from the 1941 prints, except for one.) One wonders which Homer himself would have preferred. I like to think that it would be the Ivins rather than the Ritchie style. For the former reveals clearly the linear integrity and the sculptural substance that made his etchings unique in American graphic art of the nineteenth century.

LLOYD GOODRICH

# Biographical Chronology

| | |
|---|---|
| 1836 | Born in Boston, February 24. |
| About 1842 | Family moved to Cambridge. |
| 1854 or 1855 | Apprenticed to J. H. Bufford, lithographer, Boston. |
| 1857 | Left Bufford February 24. Began free-lance illustration. |
| 1859 | Moved in autumn to New York, which remained his winter home until the 1880's. |
| 1859–61 | Attended a drawing school in Brooklyn, probably 1860. Studied in National Academy of Design night school about 1861. |
| 1861 | Moved to New York University Building, Washington Square. Covered Lincoln's inauguration. Visited the Army of the Potomac outside Washington, October. Studied painting briefly with Frédéric Rondel. |
| 1862 | On the Peninsular Campaign, Virginia, April 1 to about early May. First adult oils, late 1862. |
| 1863–65 | Occasional trips to the front. War paintings and illustrations. Rural paintings began in 1864. |
| 1864 | Elected Associate of the National Academy. |
| 1865 | Elected National Academician. |
| 1865–67 | Less active as illustrator. |
| 1866 | Sailed for France, late 1866. |

| 1867 | In France until fall. |
| 1868–74 | Active as illustrator of magazines and books. |
| 1868–69 | Visited White Mountains, both summers. |
| 1870 | Visited Adirondacks. |
| 1872 | Moved to Tenth Street Studios, New York. |
| 1873 | At Gloucester, Mass., June and July; first watercolor series. |
| 1874 | In Adirondacks, June. |
| 1875 | Last illustration in *Harper's Weekly*. In Virginia. Oils of Negro subjects, 1875–79. |
| 1878 | Summer at Houghton Farm, Mountainville, N. Y. |
| 1880 | Summer at Gloucester. |
| 1881 | To England, spring; settled near Tynemouth; watercolors and drawings. Possibly returned to America, winter of 1881–82. |
| 1882 | In England by spring. Watercolors and drawings at Tynemouth. Returned to America, November. |
| 1883 | Large watercolors based on English sketches. At Atlantic City, N. J., early summer; conceived ideas for "The Life Line" and "Undertow." Settled in summer in Prout's Neck, Maine, his home thenceforth. |
| 1884 | Began etching of "The Life Line." Trip with a fishing fleet; drawings, and ideas for "Eight Bells," "The Fog Warning," "The Herring Net," and "Lost on the Grand Banks." To Nassau, Bahamas, December. |
| 1885 | In Nassau, January and February. In Santiago de Cuba, March. |
| 1886 | In Florida, January. |

| | |
|---|---|
| 1886–89 | Seven etchings, 1886–89. No oils dated 1887–89. |
| 1889 | In Adirondacks, summer and early fall. |
| 1890 | In Florida, probably early in year. |
| 1891–92 | In Adirondacks, summer and early fall of both years. |
| 1894 | In Adirondacks, June. |
| 1895 | In Quebec, August and September. |
| 1897 | In Quebec, summer. |
| 1898–99 | In Nassau, December 1898, January and February 1899. In Bermuda, December 1899 into early 1900. |
| 1900 | In Adirondacks, June. |
| 1901 | Probably visited Bermuda. |
| 1902 | In Quebec, August. |
| 1903 | To Florida, December through February 1904. |
| 1904 | To Florida, December through January 1905. |
| 1906 | Long illness, summer. No new works from fall 1905 to fall 1908. |
| 1908 | Suffered paralytic stroke, May. To Adirondacks, June and July. |
| 1910 | Died at Prout's Neck, September 29. |

# Homer Exhibitions Featuring Prints

January 1930.
Goodspeed's Book Shop, Boston.
"Wood-engravings from Drawings
by Winslow Homer."

One hundred and nineteen wood-engravings.

June 17–August 1, 1936.
Detroit Institute of Arts, Russell A. Alger House,
Grosse Point Farms, Mich.
"Watercolors, Etchings and Woodcuts
by Winslow Homer."

Three etchings ("The Life Line," "Eight Bells,"
"Perils of the Sea"), 17 wood-engravings,
9 watercolors.

June 25–August 2, 1936.
Museum of Fine Arts, Boston.
"Exhibition of Work by Winslow Homer
and John La Farge."

Four etchings ("The Life Line," "Saved,"
"Eight Bells," "Mending the Tears"),
22 wood-engravings, 10 lithographs, 7 books,
30 watercolors, 13 drawings.

September 24–October 25, 1936.
New England Museums Association,
Addison Gallery of American Art,
Andover, Mass.
"Winslow Homer:
Watercolors, Prints and Drawings."

One etching ("Eight Bells"), wood-engravings
(unlisted), 6 lithographs, 29 watercolors and
6 drawings.

December 15, 1936–January 15, 1937.
Whitney Museum of American Art, New York.
"Winslow Homer Centenary Exhibition."

Five etchings ("The Life Line," "Eight Bells,"
"Perils of the Sea," "Mending the Nets,"
"Fly Fishing"), 47 wood-engravings, 35 oils,
64 watercolors, 18 drawings.

July 1939–January 1940.
Worcester Art Museum and American
Antiquarian Society, Worcester, Mass.
"Early New England Printmakers."

Six lithographs ("Campaign Sketches") and
24 lithographed cards ("Life in Camp").

October 14–November 2, 1940.
Robert C. Vose Galleries, Boston.

Two etchings ("Fly Fishing," "Mending the Tears"), 200 wood-engravings, 15 music covers, 5 lithographs, 3 line engravings, 20 books.

November 16–December 17, 1944.
Worcester Art Museum, Worcester, Mass.
"Winslow Homer."

Four etchings ("Eight Bells," "Perils of the Sea," "Mending the Tears," "Saved"), 39 wood-engravings, 6 lithographs ("Campaign Sketches"), 1 music cover, 2 book illustrations, 28 oils, 55 watercolors, 16 drawings.

February 1951.
Smith College Museum of Art,
Northampton, Mass.
"Winslow Homer, Illustrator."

Thirty-three wood-engravings, 20 oils, 9 watercolors, 9 drawings.

September–October 1953.
Behn-Moore Gallery, Cambridge, Mass.

Ten etchings ("Eight Bells," "Undertow," "Saved" [early plate], "Saved" [later plate, final state], "A Voice from the Cliffs" [proof state], "A Voice from the Cliffs" [final state], "Mending the Tears" [early proof], "Mending the Tears" [second proof], "Fly Fishing"), 1 oil, 12 watercolors, 3 drawings, 12 tiles.

April 14–June 6, 1955.
Wadsworth Atheneum, Hartford, Conn.
"Off for the Holidays."

Fourteen wood-engravings, 3 oils, 3 watercolors.

November 23, 1958–January 4, 1959.
National Gallery of Art, Washington, D.C.
"Winslow Homer:
a Retrospective Exhibition."

Two etchings ("Eight Bells," "Perils of the Sea"), 17 wood-engravings, 3 lithographs, 6 book illustrations, 79 oils, 100 watercolors, 30 drawings, 12 tiles.

August 15–September 15, 1959.
Adirondack Museum,
Blue Mountain Lake, N.Y.
"Winslow Homer in the Adirondacks."

Five wood-engravings, 1 oil, 23 watercolors.

Summer 1961.
Sterling and Francine Clark Art Institute,
Williamstown, Mass.
"Exhibit Sixteen: Winslow Homer."

Four etchings ("Eight Bells," "The Life Line," "Mending the Tears," "Perils of the Sea"), 9 wood-engravings, 2 music covers, 1 heliotype, 10 oils, 11 watercolors.

| | |
|---|---|
| March 2–24, 1962. International Arts Guild of the Bahamas, Government House, Nassau. "Winslow Homer." | Two etchings ("The Life Line," "Perils of the Sea"), 20 wood-engravings, 18 watercolors. |
| June 29–August 22, 1963. Storm King Art Center, Mountainville, N.Y. "Winslow Homer in New York State." | Seven wood-engravings, 12 oils, 46 watercolors. |
| September 6–October 8, 1963. Westmoreland County Museum of Art, Greensburg, Pa. "American Artists as Printmakers." | Three etchings ("Eight Bells," "Mending the Nets," "The Life Line"), 18 wood-engravings, 2 oils and 3 drawings. |
| October 11–December 1, 1963. The University of Arizona Art Gallery, Tucson, Arizona. "Yankee Painter: A Retrospective Exhibition of Oils, Watercolors and Graphics by Winslow Homer." | Three etchings ("Eight Bells," "Mending the Tears," "Fly Fishing"), 7 wood-engravings, 41 oils, 79 watercolors, 9 drawings. |
| April 16–May 30, 1966. The Picture Decorator, Inc., New York. "Winslow Homer: Original Wood Block Engravings, 1857–1875." | One hundred and fifty wood-engravings. |
| Summer 1966. Bowdoin College Museum of Art, Brunswick, Maine. "Winslow Homer at Prout's Neck." | Five etchings ("The Life Line," "Saved," "Mending the Tears," "A Voice from the Cliffs," "Fly Fishing"), 17 oils, 22 watercolors, 1 drawing. |
| April 15–June 3, 1967. The Picture Decorator, Inc., New York. "Winslow Homer: Original Wood Block Engravings, 1857–1875." | Two hundred wood-engravings. |

# Lenders to the Exhibition

Addison Gallery of American Art, Phillips
Academy, Andover
American Antiquarian Society, Worcester
The Art Institute of Chicago
Miss Lucy M. Bostwick, Haverford
Bowdoin College Museum of Art, Brunswick
The Butler Institute of American Art,
Youngstown
Cooper-Hewitt Museum of Design,
Smithsonian Institution
Mr. and Mrs. Lloyd Goodrich, New York
Mr. Donald H. Karshan, New York
Kovler Gallery: Chicago
Dr. and Mrs. Irving Levitt, Southfield
The Library of Congress
The Metropolitan Museum of Art, New York
Museum of Fine Arts, Boston
Museum of the City of New York
Philadelphia Museum of Art
Mr. William J. Poplack, Birmingham
Sterling and Francine Clark Art Institute,
Williamstown
Mrs. David B. Trammell, Fort Worth
Whitney Museum of American Art, New York

# Catalogue

In addition to Homer's lithographs, etchings and wood-engraved illustrations, the exhibition includes a selection of oils, watercolors and drawings which are related to them, represented by the works themselves or by photographs. These related works are designated by a letter following the number: i.e., No. 96 is the etching "Eight Bells," and 96A is the painting "Eight Bells" on which the etching was based.

Measurements are in inches, height preceding width. Etching measurements are of the plate. For the lithographs, "Union Pond, Williamsburgh, Long Island" and "Massachusetts Senate," measurements are of the printed image, including captions; dimensions of the sheet music covers, "Campaign Sketches" and "Life in Camp," are of the sheet of paper or the card. Wood-engraving measurements are of the picture image, not including the caption.

### Lithographs and Works Related to Them

1 The Ratcatcher's Daughter. Probably 1855.
(Pl. 1)
Lithographed sheet-music cover,
$13^1/_4 \times 10$.
Published by Oliver Ditson, Boston. J. H. Bufford's Lith., Boston. Based on the cover of

this song published in London (# 1A). Homer made considerable changes in his version.
Lent by The Metropolitan Museum of Art, Dick Fund, 1936.

1A The Ratcatcher's Daughter. c. 1855.
Wood-engraved sheet-music cover, by
W. A. Barrett.
Published by Davidson, London.

2 The Wheelbarrow Polka. 1856.
Lithographed sheet-music cover,
$13^1/_4 \times 10^1/_8$.
(From a photograph by Turner & Cutting.)
Published by Oliver Ditson, Boston.
J. H. Bufford's Lith., Boston.
Lent by The Metropolitan Museum of Art, Dick Fund, 1936.

3 Minnie Clyde, Kitty Clyde's Sister. 1857.
(Pl. 2)
Lithographed sheet-music cover,
$13^1/_8 \times 9^5/_8$.
Published by Oliver Ditson & Co., Boston.
J. H. Bufford's Lith., Boston.
Lent by The Metropolitan Museum of Art, Dick Fund, 1936.

4 Massachusetts Senate. 1856. (Pl. 3)
$21^7/_8 \times 27$.

Signed in stone, r. ctr.: "W Homer".
Published by James M. Usher, Boston.
J. H. Bufford's Lith.
Lent by the Library of Congress.

5   Union Pond, Williamsburgh, Long Island.
Probably 1862.   (Pl. 4)
$18^3/_4 \times 26^7/_8$.
Unsigned. Lithographed by Thomas & Eno,
New York.
Lent by the Museum of the City of New York.

6–12   Campaign Sketches.   "Del. and Drawn on
Stone by Winslow Homer.   Part I, contain-
ing 6 Plates."   1863.
Over-all page size of each, $14 \times 10^7/_8$.
Published by L. Prang & Co., Boston.

6   Title-page: Campaign Sketches.   (Pl. 13)
Signed l. r.: "H".
Lent by the Museum of Fine Arts, Boston.

7   The Baggage Train.   (Pl. 16)
Signed l. r.: "HOMER".
Lent by the American Antiquarian Society.

7A   The Baggage Train (Sketch).   Probably 1862.
(Pl. 15)
Pencil and wash, $9^1/_2 \times 6^3/_4$.
Lent by Cooper-Hewitt Museum of Design,
Smithsonian Institution.

8   The Coffee Call.   (Pl. 14)
Signed l. r.: "HW".
Lent by the American Antiquarian Society.

9   Foraging.   (Pl. 18)
Signed l. l.: "W HOMER DEL".

Lent by the Addison Gallery of American
Art, Phillips Academy.

10   The Letter for Home.   (Pl. 19)
Signed l. l.: "H".
Lent by the Philadelphia Museum of Art.

11   Our Jolly Cook.   (Pl. 17)
Signed l. l.: "HOMER Del".
Lent by the American Antiquarian Society.

12   A Pass Time.   Cavalry Rest.   (Pl. 20)
Signed l. r.: "WH".
Lent by the Addison Gallery of American
Art, Phillips Academy.

13–36   Life in Camp.   1864.
24 souvenir cards, each $4^1/_8 \times 2^7/_{16}$, with two
envelopes titled "Life in Camp. Part 1" and
"Life in Camp. Part 2." Published by
L. Prang & Co., Boston.
23 cards lent by The Butler Institute of
American Art; "Hard Tack" lent by the
American Antiquarian Society.

13–24   Part 1:   Building Castles; The Guard House
(signed l. l.: "WH"); Hard Tack; Late for
Roll Call; Riding on a Rail (signed l. r.: "H");
A Shell is Coming; Stuck in the Mud (signed
l. l.: "H"); Surgeons Call; Tossing in a
Blanket; An Unwelcome Visit; Upset His
Coffee; Water Call.   (Pl. 21 and 22)

25–36   Part 2: A Deserter; Drummer; Extra
Ration; The Field Barber; Fording; The
Girl He Left Behind Him; Good Bye; Home
on a Furlough; In the Trenches; Our Special;
The Rifle Pit; Teamster.   (Pl. 23 and 24)

*Wood-engravings and Works Related to Them*

The place of publication was New York, except for *Every Saturday* and *Our Young Folks*, published in Boston.

Illustrations in *Harper's Weekly* (designated *HW*), unless otherwise described, are single-page, approximately $9 \times 13^3/_4$ inches (not including the caption).

Eleven of the wood-engravings are lent by Donald H. Karshan, fifteen by Mr. and Mrs. Lloyd Goodrich, and twenty-three by the Whitney Museum of American Art.

37  Husking the Corn in New England. *HW*, Nov. 13, 1858. (Pl. 5)

38  Skating on the Ladies' Skating-pond in the Central Park, New York. *HW*, Jan. 28, 1860. (Pl. 6)
$13^3/_4 \times 20^1/_8$.

39  A Bivouac Fire on the Potomac. *HW*, Dec. 21, 1861. (Pl. 11)
$13^3/_4 \times 20^1/_8$.

40  The War for the Union, 1862—A Cavalry Charge. *HW*, July 5, 1862. (Pl. 7)
$13^3/_4 \times 20^5/_8$.

41  The War for the Union, 1862—A Bayonet Charge. *HW*, July 12, 1862. (Pl. 8)
$13^3/_4 \times 20^5/_8$.

42  The Army of the Potomac—A Sharpshooter on Picket Duty. *HW*, Nov. 15, 1862. (Pl. 10)

43  The Approach of the British Pirate "Alabama." *HW*, April 25, 1863. (Pl. 9)

44  The Great Russian Ball at the Academy of Music, November 5, 1863. *HW*, Nov. 21, 1863. (Pl. 12)
$13^1/_8 \times 20^1/_4$.

45  Our National Winter Exercise—Skating. *Frank Leslie's Illustrated Newspaper*, Jan. 13, 1866. (Pl. 25)
$14^3/_8 \times 20^7/_8$.
Lent by the Museum of Fine Arts, Boston.

46  Swinging on a Birch-tree. *Our Young Folks*, June 1867. (Pl. 33)
$5^7/_8 \times 3^5/_8$.

47  The Bird Catchers. *Our Young Folks*, Aug. 1867. (Pl. 34)
$3^5/_8 \times 5^7/_8$.

48  A Parisian Ball—Dancing at the Mabille, Paris. *HW*, Nov. 23, 1867. (Pl. 27)

49  A Parisian Ball—Dancing at the Casino. *HW*, Nov. 23, 1867. (Pl. 28)

50  Homeward-bound. *HW*, Dec. 21, 1867. (Pl. 30)
$13^1/_2 \times 20^1/_2$.

51  Art-students and Copyists in the Louvre Gallery, Paris. *HW*, Jan. 11, 1868. (Pl. 29)

52  "Winter"—A Skating Scene. *HW*, Jan. 25, 1868. (Pl. 31)

53  Watching the Crows. *Our Young Folks*, June 1868. (Pl. 35)
$5^7/_8 \times 3^5/_8$.

54 The Strawberry Bed. *Our Young Folks*, July 1868. (Pl. 38)
$3^5/_8 \times 5^7/_8$.

55 Green Apples. *Our Young Folks*, August 1868. (Pl. 36)
$5^7/_8 \times 3^5/_8$.

56 Christmas Belles. *HW*, Jan. 2, 1869. (Pl. 32)

57 Waiting for Calls on New Year's Day. *Harper's Bazaar*, Jan. 2, 1869. (Pl. 26)
$9 \times 13^3/_4$.
Lent by The Metropolitan Museum of Art, Dick Fund, 1933.

58 Winter at Sea—Taking in Sail off the Coast. *HW*, Jan. 16, 1869. (Pl. 58)

59 The Summit of Mount Washington. *HW*, July 10, 1869. (Pl. 41)

59A The Bridle Path, Mount Washington. 1868. (Pl. 39)
Oil, $24 \times 38$.
Owned by the Sterling and Francine Clark Art Institute.

59B Mount Washington. 1869. (Pl. 40)
Oil, $16 \times 24^1/_8$.
Owned by the Art Institute of Chicago.

60 The Beach at Long Branch. *Appleton's Journal of Literature, Science and Art*, Aug. 21, 1869. (Pl. 43)
$12^7/_8 \times 19^9/_{16}$.

60A Girl. Probably 1869. (Pl. 42)
Crayon, $12^1/_2 \times 5^5/_8$.
Lent by Cooper-Hewitt Museum of Design, Smithsonian Institution.

61 The Fishing Party. *Appleton's Journal of Literature, Science and Art*, Oct. 2, 1869. (Pl. 45)
$9 \times 12^5/_8$.

61A Sketch for "The Fishing Party." Probably 1869. (Pl. 44)
Pencil, $6 \times 8^3/_4$.
Lent by Cooper-Hewitt Museum of Design, Smithsonian Institution.

62 Tenth Commandment. *HW*, March 12, 1870. (Pl. 47)
$10^3/_4 \times 8^1/_2$.
Lent by The Metropolitan Museum of Art, Dick Fund, 1929.

62A Tenth Commandment. 1870. (Pl. 46)
Pencil, $11^3/_4 \times 9^1/_2$.
Lent by Mr. William J. Poplack.

63 Spring Blossoms. *HW*, May 21, 1870. (Pl. 48)

64 The Dinner Horn. *HW*, June 11, 1870. (Pl. 37)

65 The Coolest Spot in New England—Summit of Mount Washington. *Harper's Bazaar*, July 23, 1870. (Pl. 49)
$13^3/_4 \times 9^1/_8$.
Lent by The Metropolitan Museum of Art, Dick Fund, 1933.

65A A Mountain Climber Resting. Probably 1868 or 1869.
Crayon and white chalk, $7^1/_8 \times 13$.
Lent by Cooper-Hewitt Museum of Design, Smithsonian Institution.

66 On the Bluff at Long Branch, at the Bathing Hour. *HW*, Aug. 6, 1870. (Pl. 51)

67 Chestnutting. *Every Saturday*, Oct. 29, 1870. (Pl. 52)
$11^3/_4 \times 8^3/_4$.

68 A Winter-morning—Shovelling Out. *Every Saturday*, Jan. 14, 1871. (Pl. 53)
$8^3/_4 \times 11^3/_4$.

69 Deer-stalking in the Adirondacks in Winter. *Every Saturday*, Jan. 21, 1871. (Pl. 54)
$8^3/_4 \times 11^3/_4$.

70 Lumbering in Winter. *Every Saturday*, Jan. 28, 1871. (Pl. 55)
$11^3/_4 \times 8^3/_4$.

71 Cutting a Figure. *Every Saturday*, Feb. 4, 1871. (Pl. 56)
$11^3/_4 \times 18^1/_2$.

72 On the Beach—Two are Company, Three are None. *HW*, Aug. 17, 1872. (Pl. 50)

73 The Wreck of the Atlantic—Cast up by the Sea. *HW*, April 26, 1873. (Pl. 60)

73A Study for "The Wreck of the Atlantic." Probably 1873. (Pl. 59)
Pencil, $3^1/_4 \times 11^1/_2$.
Lent by Mrs. David B. Trammell.

74 The Noon Recess. *HW*, June 28, 1873. (Pl. 57)

75 The Bathers. *HW*, Aug. 2, 1873. (Pl. 62)

76 The Nooning. *HW*, Aug. 16, 1873. (Pl. 61)

77 Sea-side Sketches—A Clam-bake. *HW*, Aug. 23, 1873. (Pl. 65)

77A A Basket of Clams. 1873. (Pl. 63)
Watercolor, $11^3/_8 \times 9^7/_8$.
Owned by Mr. Stowell Rounds.

77B The Clambake. 1873. (Pl. 64)
Watercolor, $8^3/_8 \times 13^7/_8$.
Owned by the Cleveland Museum of Art.

78 Snap-the-whip. *HW*, Sept. 20, 1873. (Pl. 68)
$13^1/_2 \times 20^1/_2$.

78A Snap the Whip. 1872. (Pl. 66)
Oil, $22^1/_4 \times 36^1/_2$.
Owned by the Butler Institute of American Art.

78B Snap-the-whip. Probably 1873. (Pl. 67)
Pencil, $8^{11}/_{16} \times 19^1/_2$.
Probably used for tracing the picture on the wood-block.
Lent by the Butler Institute of American Art.

79 Gloucester Harbor. *HW*, Sept. 27, 1873. (Pl. 71)

79A Seven Boys in a Dory. July 1873. (Pl. 69)
Watercolor, $9^1/_2 \times 13^1/_2$.
Owned by Mrs. Norman B. Woolworth.

79B Boys in a Dory. 1873. (Pl. 70)
Watercolor, $9^1/_2 \times 13^1/_2$.
Owned by Mrs. William C. Knudtsen.

80 Ship-building, Gloucester Harbor. *HW*,
Oct. 11, 1873. (Pl. 75)

80A Ship-building at Gloucester. 1871. (Pl. 72)
Oil, $13^1/_2 \times 19^3/_4$.
Owned by Smith College Museum of Art.

80B Boys on a Beach. Probably 1873. (Pl. 73)
Watercolor, $5^1/_2 \times 13^3/_8$.
Owned by John Davis Hatch, Jr.

80C The Boat Builders. 1873. (Pl. 74)
Oil, $6 \times 10^1/_4$.
Owned by The Art Association of Indianapolis / John Herron Museum of Art.

81 "Dad's Coming!" *HW*, Nov. 1, 1873.
(Pl. 76)

82 The Last Days of Harvest. *HW*, Dec. 6,
1873. (Pl. 77)

83 The Morning Bell. *HW*, Dec. 13, 1873.
(Pl. 79)

84 Station-house Lodgers. *HW*, Feb. 7, 1874.
(Pl. 78)

85 Raid on a Sand-swallow Colony—"How
Many Eggs?" *HW*, June 13, 1874. (Pl. 81)

86 Gathering Berries. *HW*, July 11, 1874.
(Pl. 83)

86A The Berry Pickers. 1873. (Pl. 82)
Watercolor, $9^1/_4 \times 13^1/_8$.
Owned by Colby College Art Museum, The
Harold T. Pulsifer Memorial Collection.

87 Waiting for a Bite. *HW*, Aug. 22, 1874.
(Pl. 80)

88 Seesaw—Gloucester, Massachusetts. *HW*,
Sept. 12, 1874. (Pl. 86)

88A The Seesaw. Probably 1873. (Pl. 84)
Watercolor, $7^1/_8 \times 13^3/_8$.
Owned by the Canajoharie Library and Art
Gallery.

88B Girls with a Lobster. June 1873. (Pl. 85)
Watercolor, $8^7/_8 \times 12^1/_4$.
Owned by the Cleveland Museum of Art.

89 The Battle of Bunker Hill—Watching the
Fight from Copp's Hill, in Boston. *HW*,
June 25, 1875.

*Etchings and Works Related to Them*

90 Girl Posing in a Chair. c. 1875. (Pl. 87)
Etching, $5^7/_8 \times 4$.
Signed in plate, l. r.: "W.H."
Lent by Miss Lucy M. Bostwick.

91 The Life Line. 1884.
Etching, $12^7/_8 \times 17^3/_4$.
Green ink. Signed in plate, l. l.: "HOMER
1884"; and l. r.: "Copyright 1884 Winslow
Homer". Inscribed in plate (not in Homer's
hand), below bottom edge, center: "Copy-

right 1887 by C. Klackner, 17 East 17th St., New York." Remarque l. r.: an anchor between two dials. Signed in margin, l. r., in pencil: "Winslow Homer". Numbered "106". Lent by The Metropolitan Museum of Art, Dick Fund, 1924.

92  The Life Line.   (Pl. 90)

Printed from the plate of #91 in 1941 by Charles S. White. Black ink.
Lent by The Metropolitan Museum of Art, Dick Fund, 1941.

92A  The Life Line.   1884.   (Pl. 89)
Oil, $28^3/_4 \times 45$.
Owned by the Philadelphia Museum of Art.

93  Study for "Undertow" and a Woman's Head. c. 1886.   (Pl. 88)
Etching, $9^3/_4 \times 6^7/_8$.
Lent by the Bowdoin College Museum of Art.

94  Undertow. c. 1886.   (Pl. 92)
Etching, $6^5/_8 \times 10$.
Signed in plate, l. l.: "HOMER SC"; and l. r.: "Copyright Winslow Homer". Not signed outside plate. Only two prints known: one formerly owned in 1939 by the late Mrs. Henry C. Valentine, Darien, Conn.; the other owned in 1941 by the Homer family. Present ownership of both unknown.

94A  Undertow.   1886.   (Pl. 91)
Oil, $30 \times 47^3/_4$.
Owned by the Sterling and Francine Clark Art Institute.

95  Eight Bells.   1887.

Etching, on parchment, $19^3/_8 \times 25$.
Signed in plate, l. l.: "HOMER Sculp" and "Winslow Homer Sculp 1887". Inscribed in plate (not in Homer's hand), below bottom edge, center: "Copyright, 1887, by C. Klackner, 17 East 17th St., N.Y." Remarque l. r.: an anchor between two dials. Signed in margin, l. r., in pencil: "Winslow Homer". Numbered "32".
Lent by The Metropolitan Museum of Art, Dick Fund, 1924.

96  Eight Bells.   (Pl. 94)
Printed from the plate of #95 in 1941 by Charles S. White.
Lent by The Metropolitan Museum of Art, Dick Fund, 1941.

96A  Eight Bells.   1886.   (Pl. 93)
Oil, $25 \times 30$.
Lent by the Addison Gallery of American Art, Phillips Academy.

97  Mending the Tears.   1888.   (Pl. 96)
Etching, $17^3/_8 \times 23$.
Signed in plate, l. r.: "Winslow Homer Sc". Inscribed in plate (not in Homer's hand), above top edge, u. l.: "Copyright 1888 by Winslow Homer N.Y."; and u. r.: "G. W. H. Ritchie Imp." Remarque l. l.: an anchor. Signed in margin, l. l., in pencil: "Winslow Homer N.A."
Lent by the Kovler Gallery: Chicago.

97A  Mending Nets; or, Far from Billingsgate. 1882.   (Pl. 95)
Watercolor, $27^1/_2 \times 19^1/_2$.
Owned by Mrs. Solton Engel.

98  Perils of the Sea.   1888.
Etching, $16^1/_2 \times 22$.
Signed in plate, l. r.: "HOMER". Inscribed in plate (not in Homer's hand), above top edge, u. l.: "G. W. H. Ritchie Imp."; and below bottom edge, center: "Copyright 1888 by C. Klackner, 17 East 17th St., New York." Remarque l. l.: an anchor. Signed in margin, l. r., in pencil: "Winslow Homer N.A."
Lent by the Kovler Gallery: Chicago.

99  Perils of the Sea.   (Pl. 98)
Printed from the plate of #98 in 1941 by Charles S. White. Additional remarque, l. l. ctr.: head of a bearded fisherman in a sou'wester hat.
Lent by The Metropolitan Museum of Art, Dick Fund, 1941.

99A  Perils of the Sea.   1881.   (Pl. 97)
Watercolor, $14^5/_8 \times 20^7/_8$.   .
Lent by the Sterling and Francine Clark Art Institute.

100  A Voice from the Cliffs.   1888.   (Pl. 100)
Etching, on parchment, $19 \times 30$.
Signed in plate, l. l.: "Winslow Homer Sc. 1888". Signed in margin, l. l., in pencil: "Winslow Homer N.A. Six copies of this etching only".
Lent by Dr. and Mrs. Irving Levitt.

101  A Voice from the Cliffs.   1888.
Etching, on paper, $19 \times 30$.
Signed in plate as in #100, but not signed by Homer in margin.
Lent by The Metropolitan Museum of Art, Gift of Richard Cole, 1966.

101A  A Voice from the Cliffs.   1883.   (Pl. 99)

Watercolor, $20^3/_4 \times 29^3/_4$.
Owned by Mrs. Charlotte Ford Niarchos.

102  Saved.   1889.   (Pl. 103)
Etching, $22^7/_8 \times 32^3/_4$.
Signed in plate, l. l.: "Winslow Homer Sc". Inscribed in plate (not in Homer's hand), above top edge, u. l.: "G.W.H. Ritchie Imp.", and u. r.: "Copyright 1889 by C. Klackner, N.Y." Signed in margin, l. r., in pencil: "Winslow Homer".
Lent by the Kovler Gallery: Chicago.

103  Saved.   1889.
Undescribed first state of #102 before additional shading.
Lent by the Bowdoin College Museum of Art.

104  Fly Fishing, Saranac Lake.   1889.
Etching, $17^1/_2 \times 22^5/_8$.
Signed in plate, l. l.: "Winslow Homer Sc 1889 Copyright". Signed in margin, l. l., in pencil: "Winslow Homer". Numbered "61".
Lent by The Metropolitan Museum of Art, Dick Fund, 1924.

105  Fly Fishing, Saranac Lake.   (Pl. 102)
Printed from the plate of #104 in 1941 by Charles S. White.
Lent by The Metropolitan Museum of Art, Dick Fund, 1941.

105A  Netting the Fish.   (Pl. 101)
Black and white watercolor, $14 \times 20$.
Signed l. r.: "Winslow Homer 1890. Copyright 1889". Probably the study for #104, post-dated by Homer when exhibited in 1890.
Lent by the Art Institute of Chicago.

Plates

1. THE RATCATCHER'S DAUGHTER. Probably 1855
Lithographed sheet-music cover. (Cat. 1)

2. MINNIE CLYDE, KITTY CLYDE'S SISTER. 1857
Lithographed sheet-music cover. (Cat. 3)

3.  MASSACHUSETTS SENATE. 1856. Lithograph. (Cat. 4)

UNION POND,

WILLIAMSBURGH, L.I.

4.   UNION POND, WILLIAMSBURGH, LONG ISLAND. Probably 1862. Lithograph. (Cat. 5)

5.  HUSKING THE CORN IN NEW ENGLAND
*Harper's Weekly*, November 13, 1858. (Cat. 37)

6. SKATING ON THE LADIES' SKATING-POND IN THE CENTRAL PARK, NEW YORK
*Harper's Weekly*, January 28, 1860. (Cat. 38)

7. THE WAR FOR THE UNION, 1862—A CAVALRY CHARGE
*Harper's Weekly*, July 5, 1862. (Cat. 40)

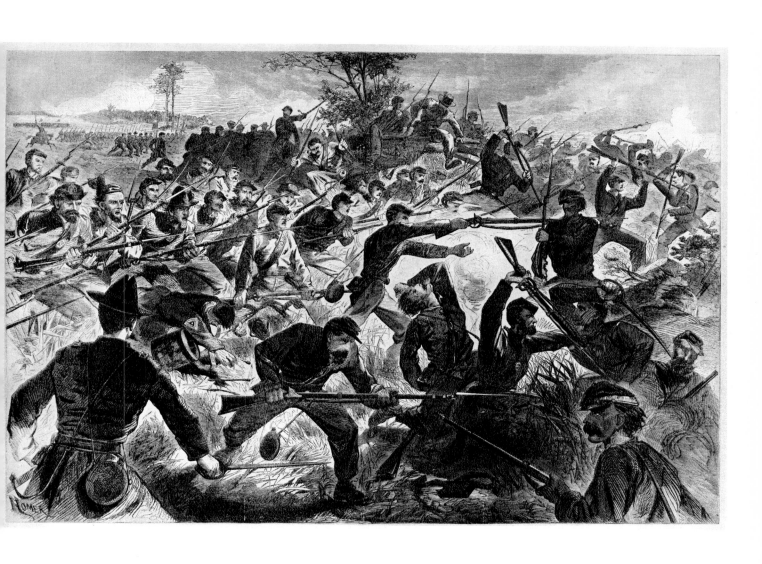

8.  THE WAR FOR THE UNION, 1862—A BAYONET CHARGE
*Harper's Weekly*, July 12, 1862. (Cat. 41)

9.  THE APPROACH OF THE BRITISH PIRATE "ALABAMA"
*Harper's Weekly*, April 25, 1863. (Cat. 43)

10.  THE ARMY OF THE POTOMAC—A SHARPSHOOTER ON PICKET DUTY
*Harper's Weekly*, November 15, 1862. (Cat. 42)

11.   A BIVOUAC FIRE ON THE POTOMAC
*Harper's Weekly*, December 21, 1861. (Cat. 39)

12.  THE GREAT RUSSIAN BALL AT THE ACADEMY OF MUSIC, NOVEMBER 5, 1863
*Harper's Weekly*, November 21, 1863. (Cat. 44)

13.   CAMPAIGN SKETCHES: TITLE-PAGE. 1863. Lithograph. (Cat. 6)

14.   CAMPAIGN SKETCHES: THE COFFEE CALL. 1863. Lithograph. (Cat. 8)

15. THE BAGGAGE TRAIN (SKETCH). Probably 1862. Pencil and wash. (Cat. 7A)

16.   CAMPAIGN SKETCHES: THE BAGGAGE TRAIN. 1863. (Cat. 7)

17.   CAMPAIGN SKETCHES: OUR JOLLY COOK. 1863. Lithograph. (Cat. 11)

18.   CAMPAIGN SKETCHES: FORAGING. 1863. Lithograph. (Cat. 9)

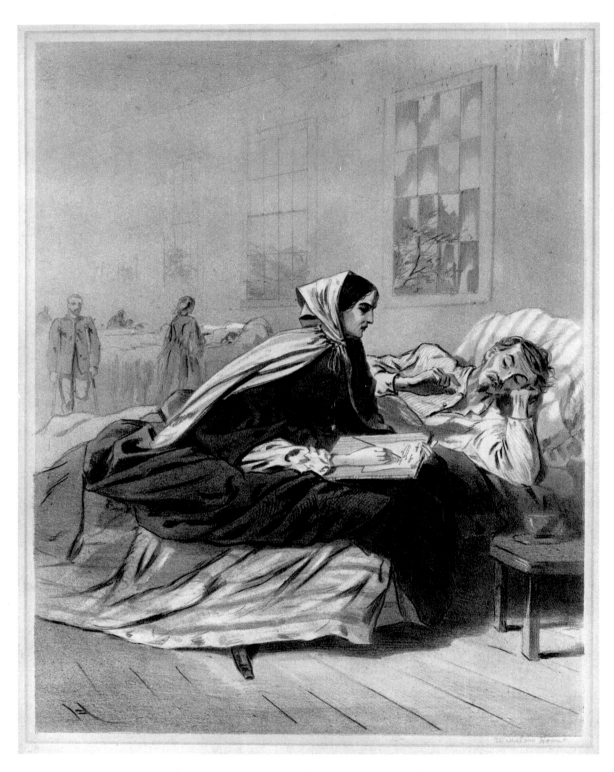

19.  CAMPAIGN SKETCHES: THE LETTER FOR HOME. 1863. Lithograph. (Cat. 10)

20. CAMPAIGN SKETCHES: A PASS TIME: CAVALRY REST. 1863. Lithograph. (Cat. 12)

BUILDING CASTLES.

STUCK IN THE MUD.

UPSET HIS COFFEE.

RIDING ON A RAIL.

HARD TACK.

A SHELL IS COMING.

21.   LIFE IN CAMP. PART 1. 1864. Lithographs. (Cat. 13—24)

TOSSING IN A BLANKET.

SURGEONS CALL.

AN UNWELCOME VISIT.

WATER CALL.

THE GUARD HOUSE.

LATE FOR ROLL CALL.

22. LIFE IN CAMP. PART 1. 1864. Lithographs. (Cat. 13—24)

HOME ON A FURLOUGH.

GOOD BYE.

THE GIRL HE LEFT BEHIND HIM.

IN THE TRENCHES.

TEAMSTER.

EXTRA RATION.

23.   LIFE IN CAMP. PART 2. 1864. Lithographs. (Cat. 25—36)

THE RIFLE PIT.

OUR SPECIAL.

THE FIELD BARBER.

DRUMMER.

DESERTER.

FORDING.

24. LIFE IN CAMP. PART 2. 1864. Lithographs. (Cat. 25—36)

25. OUR NATIONAL WINTER EXERCISE—SKATING
*Frank Leslie's Illustrated Newspaper*, January 13, 1866. (Cat. 45)

26. WAITING FOR CALLS ON NEW YEAR'S DAY
*Harper's Bazaar*, January 2, 1869. (Cat. 57)

27.  A PARISIAN BALL—DANCING AT THE MABILLE, PARIS
*Harper's Weekly*, November 23, 1867. (Cat. 48)

28. A PARISIAN BALL—DANCING AT THE CASINO
*Harper's Weekly*, November 23, 1867. (Cat. 49)

29.  ART-STUDENTS AND COPYISTS IN THE LOUVRE GALLERY, PARIS
*Harper's Weekly*, January 11, 1868. (Cat. 51)

30. HOMEWARD-BOUND
*Harper's Weekly*, December 21, 1867. (Cat. 50)

31. "WINTER"—A SKATING SCENE
*Harper's Weekly*, January 25, 1868. (Cat. 52)

32. CHRISTMAS BELLES
*Harper's Weekly*, January 2, 1869. (Cat. 56)

33.   SWINGING ON A BIRCH-TREE
*Our Young Folks,* June 1867. (Cat. 46)

34. THE BIRD CATCHERS
*Our Young Folks*, August 1867. (Cat. 47)

35.   WATCHING THE CROWS
*Our Young Folks*, June 1868. (Cat. 53)

36.   GREEN APPLES
*Our Young Folks*, August 1868. (Cat. 55)

37.  THE DINNER HORN
*Harper's Weekly*, June 11, 1870. (Cat. 64)

38.   THE STRAWBERRY BED
*Our Young Folks*, July 1868. (Cat. 54)

Top: 39. THE BRIDLE PATH, MOUNT WASHINGTON. 1868. Oil. (Cat. 59A)
Bottom: 40. MOUNT WASHINGTON. 1869. Oil. (Cat. 59B)

41. THE SUMMIT OF MOUNT WASHINGTON
*Harper's Weekly*, July 10, 1869. (Cat. 59)

42.   GIRL. Probably 1869. Crayon. (Cat. 60A)

43.   THE BEACH AT LONG BRANCH
*Appleton's Journal of Literature, Science and Art*, August 21, 1869. (Cat. 60)

44.   Sketch for THE FISHING PARTY
Probably 1869. Pencil. (Cat. 61A)

45.   THE FISHING PARTY
*Appleton's Journal of Literature, Science and Art*, October 2, 1869, (Cat. 61)

46. TENTH COMMANDMENT. 1870. Pencil. (Cat. 62A)

47.   TENTH COMMANDMENT
*Harper's Weekly*, March 12, 1870. (Cat. 62)

48.   SPRING BLOSSOMS
*Harper's Weekly*, May 21, 1870. (Cat. 63)

49.   THE COOLEST SPOT IN NEW ENGLAND—SUMMIT OF MOUNT WASHINGTON
*Harper's Bazaar*, July 23, 1870. (Cat. 65)

50.   ON THE BEACH—TWO ARE COMPANY, THREE ARE NONE
*Harper's Weekly*, August 17, 1872. (Cat. 72)

51. ON THE BLUFF AT LONG BRANCH, AT THE BATHING HOUR
*Harper's Weekly*, August 6, 1870. (Cat. 66)

52. CHESTNUTTING
*Every Saturday*, October 29, 1870. (Cat. 67)

53.   A WINTER-MORNING—SHOVELLING OUT
*Every Saturday*, January 14, 1871. (Cat. 68)

54.   DEER-STALKING IN THE ADIRONDACKS IN WINTER
*Every Saturday*, January 21, 1871. (Cat. 69)

55. LUMBERING IN WINTER
*Every Saturday*, January 28, 1871. (Cat. 70)

56.   CUTTING A FIGURE
*Every Saturday*, February 4, 1871. (Cat. 71)

57.  THE NOON RECESS
*Harper's Weekly,* June 28, 1873. (Cat. 74)

58. WINTER AT SEA—TAKING IN SAIL OFF THE COAST
*Harper's Weekly*, January 16, 1869. (Cat. 58)

Top: 59. Study for THE WRECK OF THE ATLANTIC. Probably 1873. Pencil. (Cat. 73A)
Bottom: 60. THE WRECK OF THE ATLANTIC—CAST UP BY THE SEA
*Harper's Weekly*, April 26, 1873. (Cat. 73)

61.   THE NOONING

*Harper's Weekly*, August 16, 1873. (Cat. 76)

62.   THE BATHERS
*Harper's Weekly*, August 2, 1873. (Cat. 75)

Top: 64.   THE CLAMBAKE. 1873. Watercolor. (Cat. 77B)
Bottom: 63.   A BASKET OF CLAMS. 1873. Watercolor. (Cat. 77A)

65.   SEA-SIDE SKETCHES—A CLAM-BAKE
*Harper's Weekly*, August 23, 1873. (Cat. 77)

Top: 66. Snap the whip. 1872. Oil. (Cat. 78A)
Bottom: 67. Snap-the-whip. Probably 1873. Pencil. (Cat. 78B)

68.   SNAP-THE-WHIP
*Harper's Weekly*, September 20, 1873. (Cat. 78)

Top: 69. SEVEN BOYS IN A DORY. 1873. Watercolor. (Cat. 79A)
Bottom: 70. BOYS IN A DORY. 1873. Watercolor. (Cat. 79B)

71. GLOUCESTER HARBOR
*Harper's Weekly*, September 27, 1873. (Cat. 79)

Above left:

72.   SHIP-BUILDING AT GLOUCESTER. 1871. Oil
(Cat. 80A)

Above:

73.   BOYS ON A BEACH. Probably 1873
Watercolor. (Cat. 80B)

Left:

74.   THE BOAT BUILDERS. 1873. Oil
(Cat. 80C)

75. SHIP-BUILDING, GLOUCESTER HARBOR
*Harper's Weekly*, October 11, 1873. (Cat. 80)

76. "Dad's coming!"
*Harper's Weekly*, November 1, 1873. (Cat. 81)

77.   THE LAST DAYS OF HARVEST
*Harper's Weekly*, December 6, 1873. (Cat. 82)

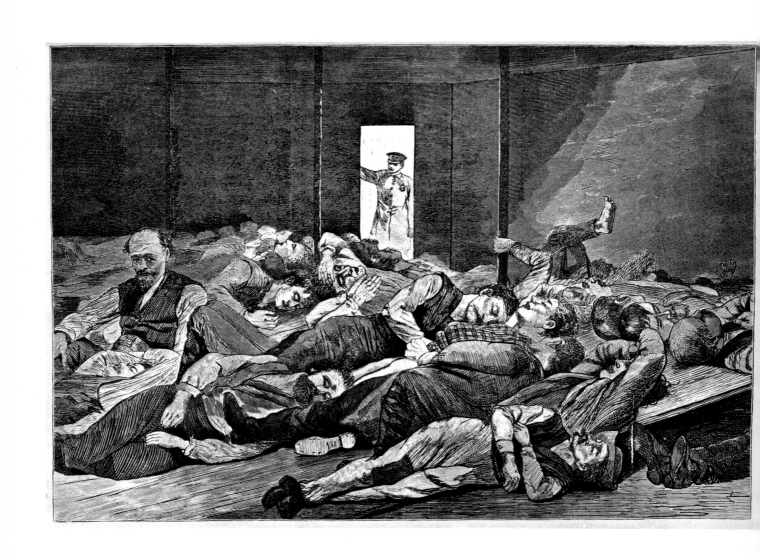

78. STATION-HOUSE LODGERS
*Harper's Weekly*, February 7, 1874. (Cat. 84)

79.  THE MORNING BELL
*Harper's Weekly*, December 13, 1873. (Cat. 83)

80.  WAITING FOR A BITE
*Harper's Weekly*, August 22, 1874. (Cat. 87)

81. RAID ON A SAND-SWALLOW COLONY—"HOW MANY EGGS?"
*Harper's Weekly*, June 13, 1874. (Cat. 85)

82. THE BERRY PICKERS. 1873. Watercolor. (Cat. 86A)

83.   GATHERING BERRIES
*Harper's Weekly*, July 11, 1874. (Cat. 86)

Top: 84. THE SEESAW. Probably 1873. Watercolor. (Cat. 88A)
Bottom: 85. GIRLS WITH A LOBSTER. 1873. Watercolor. (Cat. 88B)

86.  Seesaw—Gloucester, Massachusetts
*Harper's Weekly*, September 12, 1874. (Cat. 88)

87.   GIRL POSING IN A CHAIR. c. 1875. Etching. (Cat. 90)

88.   Study for UNDERTOW and A WOMAN'S HEAD. c. 1886. Etching. (Cat. 93)

89.   THE LIFE LINE. 1884. Oil. (Cat. 92A)

90.   THE LIFE LINE. 1884. Etching. (Cat. 92)

91.   UNDERTOW. 1886. Oil. (Cat. 94A)

92.   UNDERTOW. c. 1886. Etching. (Cat. 94)

93.   EIGHT BELLS. 1886. Oil. (Cat. 96A)

94.   EIGHT BELLS. 1887. Etching. (Cat. 96)

95.   MENDING NETS; OR, FAR FROM BILLINGSGATE. 1882. Watercolor. (Cat. 97A)

96.   Mending the tears. 1888. Etching. (Cat. 97)

97. PERILS OF THE SEA. 1881. Watercolor. (Cat. 99A)

98.  PERILS OF THE SEA. 1888. Etching. (Cat. 99)

99.   A VOICE FROM THE CLIFFS. 1883. Watercolor. (Cat. 101A)

100.   A VOICE FROM THE CLIFFS. 1888. Etching. (Cat. 100)

101.   NETTING THE FISH. Probably 1889. Watercolor. (Cat. 105A)

102.   FLY FISHING, SARANAC LAKE. 1889. Etching. (Cat. 105)

103.   SAVED. 1889. Etching. (Cat. 102)

# Selected Bibliography

*The place of publication is New York unless otherwise noted.*

## MONOGRAPHS

Beam, Philip C. *Winslow Homer at Prout's Neck*. Little, Brown & Co., Boston, 1966.

Burroughs, Louise. *Winslow Homer, A Picture Book*. The Metropolitan Museum of Art, 1939.

Cox, Kenyon. *Winslow Homer*. Privately printed, 1914.

Downes, William Howe. *The Life and Works of Winslow Homer*. Houghton, Mifflin Co., Boston and New York, 1911.

Flexner, James Thomas. *The World of Winslow Homer*. Time, Inc., 1966.

Gardner, Albert Ten Eyck. *Winslow Homer*. Clarkson N. Potter, Inc., 1961.

Goodrich, Lloyd. *Winslow Homer*. Published for the Whitney Museum of American Art by the Macmillan Co., 1944.

*Winslow Homer*. (Metropolitan Museum of Art Miniatures), The Metropolitan Museum of Art, 1956.

*Winslow Homer*. George Braziller, Inc., 1959.

Pousette-Dart, Nathaniel. *Winslow Homer*. Frederick A. Stokes Co., 1923.

Watson, Forbes. *Winslow Homer*. Crown Publishers, 1942.

## BOOKS

Barker, Virgil. *American Painting*. The Macmillan Co., 1950.

Baur, John I. H. *American Painting in the Nineteenth Century*. Frederick A. Praeger, Inc., 1953.

Benjamin, S. G. W. *Art in America*. Harper & Brothers, 1880.

Burroughs, Alan. *Limners and Likenesses*. Harvard University Press, Cambridge, Mass., 1936.

Caffin, Charles H. *American Masters of Painting*. Doubleday, Page & Co., 1902.

*Story of American Painting*. Frederick A. Stokes Co., 1907.

Cahill, Holger, and Barr, Alfred H., Jr. *Art in America in Modern Times*. Reynal & Hitchcock, 1934.

Cortissoz, Royal. *American Artists*. Charles Scribner's Sons, 1923.

Downes, William Howe. *Twelve Great Artists.* Boston, 1900.

Eliot, Alexander. *Three Hundred Years of American Painting.* Time, Inc., 1957.

Flexner, James Thomas. *The Pocket History of American Painting.* Pocket Books, 1950.

Goodrich, Lloyd. *American Watercolor and Winslow Homer.* Walker Art Center, Minneapolis, Minn., 1945.

Hartley, Marsden. *Adventures in the Arts.* Boni & Liveright, 1921.

Isham, Samuel. *History of American Painting.* The Macmillan Co., 1905.

Larkin, Oliver W. *Art and Life in America.* Holt, Rinehart & Winston, Inc., 1949, 1960.

Mather, Frank Jewett, Jr. *Estimates in Art, Series II.* Henry Holt & Co., Inc., 1931.

Myers, Bernard. *Fifty Great Artists.* Bantam Books, 1953.

Phillips, Duncan. *A Collection in the Making.* Phillips Memorial Gallery, Washington, 1926.

Richardson, Edgar P. *American Romantic Painting.* E. Weyhe, Inc., 1944.

*Painting in America.* Thomas Y. Crowell Co., 1956, 1965.

Sheldon, George W. *American Painters.* D. Appleton & Co., 1879.

*Hours with Art and Artists.* 1882.

Sherman, Frederic Fairchild. *American Painters of Yesterday and Today.* Privately printed, 1919.

Tuckerman, Henry T. *Book of the Artists: American Artist Life.* G. P. Putnam, 1867.

Van Rensselaer, Mrs. Schuyler. *Six Portraits.* Houghton, Mifflin Co., Boston and New York, 1889.

Walker, John. *Paintings from America.* Penguin Press, Hammondsworth, England, 1951.

Walker, John, and James, Macgill. *Great American Paintings from Smibert to Bellows 1729–1924.* Oxford University Press, London and New York, 1943.

Weitenkampf, Frank. *American Graphic Art.* The Macmillan Co., 1912.

## EXHIBITION CATALOGUES

Adirondack Museum: *Winslow Homer in the Adirondacks*, 1959. Text by James W. Fosburgh.

Bowdoin College Museum of Art: *Winslow Homer at Prout's Neck*, 1966. Text by Philip C. Beam.

The Museum of Modern Art, N. Y.: *Homer, Ryder, Eakins*, 1930. "Winslow Homer" by Frank Jewett Mather, Jr.

National Gallery of Art and The Metropolitan Museum of Art: *Winslow Homer, a Retrospective Exhibition*, 1958–59. Text by Albert Ten Eyck Gardner.

New England Museums Association: *Winslow Homer, Watercolors, Prints and Drawings*, 1936.

Smith College Museum of Art: *Winslow Homer, Illustrator*, 1951. Text by Mary Bartlett Cowdrey.

Sterling and Francine Clark Art Institute: *Winslow Homer*, 1961.

Storm King Art Center: *Winslow Homer in New York State*, 1963. Text by Lloyd Goodrich.

Virginia Museum of Fine Arts: *Homer and the Sea*, 1964. Text by Lloyd Goodrich.

Whitney Museum of American Art: *Winslow Homer Centenary Exhibition,* 1936. Text by Lloyd Goodrich.

Wildenstein & Co., N. Y.: *Winslow Homer*, 1947. Text by Lloyd Goodrich.

## PERIODICALS

Bolton, Theodore: "Art of Winslow Homer: An Estimate in 1932," *Fine Arts*, v. 18, Feb. 1932, p. 23–55.

"Watercolors by Homer: Critique and Catalogue," *Fine Arts*, v. 18, Apr. 1932, p. 16–20, 50, 52, 54.

Brinton, Christian: "Winslow Homer," *Scribner's Magazine*, v. 49, Jan. 1911, p. 9–23.

Chase, J. Eastman: "Some Recollections of Winslow Homer," *Harper's Weekly*, v. 54, Oct. 22, 1910, p. 13.

Cox, Kenyon: "Art of Winslow Homer," *Scribner's Magazine*, v. 56, Sept. 1914, p. 377–388.

Fosburgh, James W.: "Winslow Homer—Artist," *New York State Conservationist*, v. 3, Aug.–Sept. 1948, p. 16–18.

Foster, Allen E.: "Check List of Illustrations by Winslow Homer," *Bulletin of the New York Public Library*, v. 40, Oct. 1936, p. 842–852.

"Check List of Illustrations by Winslow Homer; A Supplement," *Bulletin of the New York Public Library*, v. 44, July 1940, p. 537–39.

Gardner, Albert Ten Eyck: "Metropolitan Homers," *Metropolitan Museum Bulletin*, v. 7, Jan. 1959, p. 132–143.

Goodrich, Lloyd: "Winslow Homer," *The Arts*, v. 6, Oct. 1924, p. 185–209.

"Winslow Homer," *Perspectives USA*, No. 14, Winter 1956, p. 44–54.

"Realism and Romanticism in Homer, Eakins and Ryder," *Art Quarterly*, v. 12, Winter 1949, p. 17–28.

"Young Winslow Homer," *Magazine of Art*, v. 37, Feb. 1944, p. 58–63.

Hathaway, Calvin S.: "Drawings by Winslow Homer in the Museum's Collections," *Chronicle of the Cooper Union Museum*, v. 1, Apr. 1936, p. 52–63.

James, Henry, Jr.: "On Some Pictures Lately Exhibited," *Galaxy*, v. 20, July 1875, p. 88–97.

Karshan, Donald H.: "American Printmaking, 1670–1968," *Art in America*, v. 56, no. 4, 1968, p. 22–55.

Katz, Leslie: "The Modernity of Winslow Homer," *Arts*, v. 33, Feb. 1959, p. 24–27.

McCausland, Elizabeth: "Winslow Homer—Graphic Artist," *Prints*, v. 7, Apr. 1937, p. 214–220.

Mather, Frank Jewett, Jr.: "Winslow Homer as a Book Illustrator," *Princeton University Library Chronicle*, v. 1, Nov. 1938.

Richardson, Edgar P.: "Winslow Homer's Drawings in Harper's Weekly," *Art in America*, v. 19, Dec. 1930, p. 38–47.

Sherman, Frederic Fairchild: "Early Oil Paintings of Winslow Homer," *Art in America*, v. 6, June 1918, p. 201–208. Reprinted in Sherman: *American Painters of Yesterday and Today*.

"Winslow Homer's Book Illustrations," *Art in America*, v. 25, Oct. 1937, p. 173–175.

Smith, Jacob Getlar: "The Watercolors of Winslow Homer," *American Artist*, v. 19, Feb. 1955, p. 19–23.

Tatham, David: "Winslow Homer and The Ratcatcher's Daughter," *The Courier* (Syracuse University), no. 28, 1967, p. 4–9.

Van Rensselaer, M. G.: "An American Artist in England," *Century Magazine*, v. 27, Nov. 1883, p. 13–21.

Watson, Forbes: "Winslow Homer," *American Magazine of Art*, v. 29, Oct. 1936, p. 625–637, 681–683.

Wehle, Harry B.: "Early Paintings by Homer," *Bulletin of the Metropolitan Museum*, v. 18, Feb. 1923, p. 38–41.

Weitenkampf, Frank: "Winslow Homer and the Wood Block," *Bulletin of the New York Public Library*, v. 36, Nov. 1932, p. 731–736.

"The Intimate Homer: Winslow Homer's Sketches," *Art Quarterly*, v. 6, Autumn 1943, p. 307–321.

Weller, Allen: "Winslow Homer's Early Illustrations," *American Magazine of Art*, v. 28, July 1935, p. 412–417.

"A Note on Winslow Homer's Drawings in Harper's Weekly," *Art in America*, v. 22, Mar. 1934, p. 76–78.

This book was set in Times type
by Brüder Rosenbaum of Vienna, Austria,
printed in monogravure and offset
by Amilcare Pizzi S. p. A. of Milano, Italy.
Design by Ulrich Ruchti.

*Cover illustration:*
*Detail of Winslow Homer's "Saved," etching.*

*Back cover illustration:*
*Winslow Homer's "Perils of the Sea," etching.*